A LOVE OFFERING

Jonathan Norton

BROADWAY PLAY PUBLISHING INC
New York
www.broadwayplaypublishing.com
info@broadwayplaypublishing.com

I0139513

A LOVE OFFERING
© Copyright 2020 Jonathan Norton

Cover photo by Jordan Fraker

First edition: April 2020
I S B N: 978-0-88145-865-7

Book design: Marie Donovan
Page make-up: Adobe InDesign
Typeface: Palatino

A LOVE OFFERING was workshopped as part of the National New Play Network Cross-Pollination Workshop at InterAct Theatre Company (Seth Rozin, Artistic Director) in Philadelphia. It was directed by Kittson O'Neill. Cross Pollination was a partnership between Kitchen Dog Theater and InterAct Theatre Company.

A LOVE OFFERING was workshopped as part of the 2018 Whither Goest Thou America: A Festival of New American Play Readings at Undermain Theatre (Katherine Owens, Founding Artistic Director; Bruce DuBose, Producing Artistic Director), directed by Dennis Raveneau.

A LOVE OFFERING received its world premiere on October 3, 2019 at Kitchen Dog Theater (Christopher Carlos & Tina Parker, Artistic Directors; Tim Johnson, Managing Director) in Dallas. The cast and creative contributors were:

T'WANA ....Whitney LaTrice Coulter
STEWART...Max Hartman
JOSIE.. Brandy McClendon Kae
MISS GEORGIA.. Rhonda Boutté
MR TURNER...Chris Messersmith

Director .... Tina Parker
Stage manager.. Sarah Duc
Set design .... Clare Floyd Devries
Light design ....Lisa Miller
Costume design ....Melissa Panzarello
Sound design.. Claire Carson
Prop design ....Cindy Ernst-Godinez
Tech director ....Lori Honeycutt
Dramaturg .... Haley Nelson

CHARACTERS & SETTING

T'WANA, *African-American female—26 years old.*
A nurse's aide at a nursing home.

STEWART, *White male—47 years old.*
Runs the family business with his younger sister.
His father lives in the nursing home where T'WANA *works.*

JOSIE, *White female—43 years old.*
STEWART'*s younger sister and business partner.*

MISS GEORGIA, *African-American female—67 years old.*
A nurse's aide at the same nursing home. T'WANA'*s play*
mama.

MR TURNER, *white—73 years old.*
STEWART *and* JOSIE'*s father.*

Dallas, TX
An Assisted Living Center.

Time: The Present

Note: A (/) indicates overlapping dialogue.

Scene One

(Lights up on a patient room at White Rock North Assisted Living Center. JOSIE stands watch at her father's bedside.)

(Her father, MR TURNER is knocked out sleep. Good drugs.)

(JOSIE's brother STEWART sits at a small table with T'WANA, a nurses' aide. She has a large bandage on her left forearm.)

(T'WANA and STEWART look through a scrapbook of photos and clippings.)

(Through the window, night pokes in.)

T'WANA: These are some really nice write-ups. Your father was a good man.

STEWART: We're very proud of him.

T'WANA: You should be.
Well, thank you for coming out and showing your concern. I appreciate that. But I gotta get back on the floor.

STEWART: Is everything okay?

T'WANA: Okay, like what?

STEWART: Your arm.

T'WANA: Oh. I'm healing, praise God.
(Chuckles)
Your daddy got me good. It's ugly under this bandage.
(Beat)
But…I'm mending.

Thanks for asking.

(T'WANA *stands to leave but* STEWART *gestures for her to stay. She hesitates, then sits.*)

STEWART: Before you go, we truly want to apologize for what our father did to you.

(STEWART *looks to* JOSIE *to chime in. She doesn't.*)

STEWART: Josie, do you have something you would like to say?

JOSIE: No. You covered everything.

(STEWART *gives her a look.*)

JOSIE: I'm sorry daddy got out of hand with you. Can I ask you a question? What happened to LaToya?

T'WANA: I don't know. They don't tell me those things.

JOSIE: Well I really liked LaToya. No offense to you.

T'WANA: None taken.

JOSIE: LaToya was really good with daddy.

T'WANA: I'm sure she was.

JOSIE: When did you start taking care of him?

T'WANA: They assigned me to him last week.

JOSIE: Do they always change people like this without notifying the family?

T'WANA: I don't know about all that.

JOSIE: I was out of town last week. But if I had known they were going to give daddy a new caretaker, I would have changed my plans.

T'WANA: I understand.

JOSIE: Daddy probably got upset because he doesn't know you.

T'WANA: Sometimes that happens. Yes.

JOSIE: Then if that's the case why would they make such a big change without giving us notice?

STEWART: Josie, that's not any of her concern.

T'WANA: Listen I really can't stay long but, I just want you to know I really like taking care of your father. We had that little incident but I didn't think nothing of it. He has alls-timers.

JOSIE: Alz—

STEWART: EXACTLY! Exactly. It's like he's a very young child.

T'WANA: Oh I understand. It's just like when my boys was babies. Talk about a handful. Double trouble I call 'em. See I got Tramaine.
(*Shows the tattoos on her neck and wrist*)
He just turned ten. He's my big boy. And Terrell. He's eight. That's my baby-baby.

STEWART: Well look at that. My sister has a tattoo.

T'WANA: Really. What is it?

JOSIE: ... ...Princess Leia with a gun.

T'WANA: I like tattoos. I got this one, too. See.

STEWART: Matthew. Six thirty-three.

T'WANA: (*Reciting from memory*) Seek first the kingdom of God and his righteousness, and all these things will be added to you.
That's my favorite.

STEWART: You know the scripture?

T'WANA: I *know* scripture. I ran B T U at my church back home.

STEWART: B T U?

T'WANA: Baptist Training Union. I was the youngest person to ever run it in the history of my church. Plus my mother was a minister. She's passed on. Gone to Glory. She didn't leave me with much. But she left me with Scripture. The Word.

STEWART: Well I think that's a lot. More than most people have.
Well good for you. So, are you from Dallas?

T'WANA: Little Rock.

STEWART: Oh. Little Rock. Josie, do we know anyone from Little Rock?

JOSIE: Not that I can recall. No.

STEWART: Well. I guess we do now.
(Beat)
So how long have you lived in Dallas?

(A woman is heard yelling, followed by an alarm ringing.)

(STEWART is startled.)

T'WANA: Oh it's okay. That's Miss Cohen.

JOSIE: Oh. Dear. There she goes again.

T'WANA: She tries to get out from time to time.

JOSIE: Her daughter says she lost her whole family at Auschwitz. And she thinks she's still there. My Lord.

STEWART: Her whole family?

JOSIE: Terrifying.

T'WANA: They say she hid in a toilet just like in that movie. Schindler's List.

STEWART: So horrific. Have you ever seen the movie?

T'WANA: I saw some of it. But I couldn't make it through. I had to stop watching.

STEWART: Yes. It's a difficult movie to watch.

T'WANA: It sure is. I don't like black and white movies. Well it was nice to meet you. I'm happy that you're nice people and you understand.

STEWART: It was lovely to meet you too. But before you go.

(STEWART *pulls out a Hallmark envelope and gives it to* T'WANA.)

STEWART: From the bottom of our hearts we apologize for the injury and insult our father caused you. And I know this isn't much but I want to offer you this as a token of our heartfelt apology.

(T'WANA opens the envelope and pulls out an Afro-Centric thank-you card.

T'WANA: (*Reads the outside of the card*) It takes a village…
(*A debit gift card is placed inside.*)
Five hundred dollars…

(JOSIE *gives* STEWART *a look.*)

STEWART: This is what God placed on my heart. It is to help with any medical bills or discomfort this might have caused you.

JOSIE: Uh…
(*She gives a "I'm sorry. I just lost your name" look.*)

T'WANA: T'Wana.

JOSIE: Do you mind giving us a moment? I need to discuss something with my brother. If you could step outside, please. It's nothing bad.

T'WANA: Well I need to get back on the floor.

JOSIE: We won't keep you long. I promise.

(T'WANA *leaves the room.*)

JOSIE: What the hell are you thinking?

STEWART: That's the amount God placed on my heart.

JOSIE: God placed on your heart to blindside your sister? Really? Stewart, we never discussed this.

STEWART: He bit her.

JOSIE: And I'm sorry that happened. But this is a nursing/ home and

STEWART: It's not a nursing home. It's an assisted living center—

JOSIE: Stewart?

STEWART: Well that's what it's called.

JOSIE: Whatever it's called, things like this happen. It's her job and we owe her nothing. Stewart, think it through. She's been injured, our father is at fault and giving her any money at all—do you know how that looks? And five hundred dollars.

STEWART: Well we have to do something. What about her medical bills?

JOSIE: Workers Comp. You know that. Stewart, think it through.

STEWART: I'm trying to do the Christian thing. I'm doing what daddy would do.

JOSIE: Daddy is the one that got us into this mess. He's the last person you should be trying to emulate.

STEWART: I'm trying to get her on our side. We need her help. Yes?

(No response)

STEWART: Jo-Jo?

JOSIE: No. You saw what she did to daddy.

STEWART: Those are two different things

JOSIE: So now we're rewarding bad behavior? And what/ about

STEWART: We'll get to the bottom of things. I promise.
But first, we have to get her on our side.
Yes?

JOSIE: *Yes.*
(Beat)
We pay enough for daddy to live here. Too much.
We shouldn't have to pay for him to be protected and
treated fairly too. We have to draw the line.

(There's a knock at the door. The door cracks open, T'WANA
pokes her head in.)

T'WANA: I need to get back on my rounds. I don't want
to get wrote up. I ain't never been wrote up, and I ain't
getting wrote up tonight. I can't keep standing out in
the hallway not doing nothing.

STEWART: Come in. Please. We're sorry.

T'WANA: *(Hesitates)* Well…I was just told I shouldn't
be meeting with y'all without Mr Water's permission.

(JOSIE grunts. If she had said a word the word would have
been "figures".)

STEWART: Why? It's just a friendly talk. Did you tell
them that we apologized?

T'WANA: Well because of the attack, they/said

JOSIE: It wasn't an attack. He doesn't know any better.

T'WANA: I didn't mean it like that. I'm just saying what
they said—

JOSIE: Who is they?

T'WANA: The nurses' station—

(JOSIE stands to leave, ready to confront the folks at the
nurse's station.)

STEWART: Josie. No. Wait. Let's handle this first. Deal
with that later.

(*Beat.* JOSIE *stops.*)

STEWART: T'Wana. Please.

(STEWART *sits.* T'WANA *sits. She looks at the scrapbook. But Josie quickly scoops it. She goes to her chair and flips through it—but mostly her attention is trained on* T'WANA.)

STEWART: T'Wana, you do not believe our father attacked you?

T'WANA: No. He not in his right mind. Is that what this is about? You want me to say he didn't attack me? He didn't attack me. I can keep the money, right?

STEWART: Of course. Yes that is for you. It is our way of thanking you for all that you do.

T'WANA: Like a love offering at church.

STEWART: Yes. A love offering.

T'WANA: That's what we gonna call it. I like that. Thank you.
(*Beat*)
Don't mean to rush, but I gotta get back to work.

STEWART: One more thing.
Uh…speaking of work, are you looking for something better

T'WANA: Huh?

STEWART: You have a high school diploma?

T'WANA: G E D.

STEWART: Give her your card.

JOSIE: Why my card?

STEWART: You work with the hiring managers.

(JOSIE *gives* T'WANA *her business card.*)

T'WANA: Turner Corporate Relocations.

STEWART: Our father started the business.
(*Nods to his sister*)
We run it now.

T'WANA: Are you offering me a job?

JOSIE: No—
I mean we don't have jobs to offer.

STEWART: But we know where the jobs are and Josie has relationships with the hiring managers. Just think how much better life would be for your sons. Starting pay at least fourteen dollars an hour. Good benefits. Mostly call center work. You interested?

T'WANA: I'll pray on it and let you know.

STEWART: Don't you want a better job?

T'WANA: Yeah. And I'm gonna get one. I'm building a good foundation here. Throw that away to start someplace new? That don't make sense to me. Besides call centers dead end. They shut those down left and right. But nursing homes ain't going nowhere. They here to stay. I mean every now and then you hear about them burning down, or flooding. You know, stuff like that. But that's different than being laid off.

STEWART: Well…there's better opportunities out there. May I ask, how much do you make here?

(JOSIE *gives* STEWART *a look.*)

T'WANA: Ten twenty-five an hour.

STEWART: Health insurance?

T'WANA: I'm working on it.

STEWART: But if you don't have health insurance then you shouldn't turn down—
How do you take care of your boys?

(STEWART *just crossed a line.*)

T'WANA: If it's serious, I take them to Parkland.
They on the CHIP program. If not, Tammy the nurse
practitioner sees them. She real nice. She doctors on me
too. She gave me my shot and treatments for the bite.

JOSIE: Same as last time?

T'WANA: Excuse me?

JOSIE: You've been bit before.

T'WANA: How do you know that?

JOSIE: One of my friends here.

T'WANA: Oh…well…it was nothing really. Mr Connor
don't have that many teeth. But your daddy got just
about all his teeth. Oooooooooh Jesus. But that's a
blessing though I suppose.

JOSIE: Do you think it might be possible that you're
doing something to provoke the bite? Inadvertently.
Not on purpose.

T'WANA: I did not do anything to harm—

JOSIE: Not harm. Provoke.

T'WANA: I treat all the residents the way I would want
somebody to treat my mama, if I put her off in a home.

JOSIE: We didn't have a choice. Daddy needs twenty-
four seven care.

T'WANA: Look, I take pity on them when they have
alls-timers.

JOSIE:	T'WANA:
It's pronounc/ed—	I know how it's pro/nounced.

JOSIE:	STEWART:
ALZHEIMER'S	JOSIE!

T'WANA: Alzzzzz –himerz. Maybe I have trouble saying it but I know what it is and I know they can't help the things they say or do.

STEWART: We're not accusing you of anything. What Josie is trying to say is that maybe he became confused and thought he needed to defend himself.

T'WANA: I didn't do anything to provoke him.

STEWART: And that's why I said confused.

JOSIE: Why did the other man bite you?

T'WANA: Mr Conner? He hate black people. I think alls-timers makes them be racist sometimes.

STEWART: Alzheimer's does not turn you into a racist.

T'WANA: Then why did your daddy call me the N-Word?

STEWART: That wasn't our father that called you that.

T'WANA: I am very sorry that your daddy is sick. And I do my best to take care of him. Now I gotta get back on the floor.
(Beat)
Anything else you need to know you should take up with Mr Waters.
(She leaves.)

JOSIE: Stewart. Why did you let her leave? You just let her walk out the door.

STEWART: Josie, what if we're barking up the wrong tree? Are you sure she's friends—

JOSIE: Yes. I'm sure. Miss Olson's daughter said she's good friends with—

STEWART: Who is Miss Olson?

JOSIE: The lady across the hall from daddy.

STEWART: I thought that was Mr Phillips.

JOSIE: He died. They moved Miss Olson to that room. Shit! Go find her! NOW!

(STEWART *pops his head out the door.*)

STEWART: She's not in the hallway.

JOSIE: Go look for her.

STEWART: She could be anywhere.

JOSIE: She couldn't have gotten that far. Black people walk slow.

STEWART: Josie.

JOSIE: What? Daddy said that all the time.

STEWART: Daddy didn't joke like that.

JOSIE: He didn't mean it as a joke. He was stating it as a fact. You remember. About the guys who worked for him.

STEWART: I don't recall him saying ugly things like that.

JOSIE: He didn't mean anything bad by it.

Stewart?

STEWART: You shouldn't say things like that.

JOSIE: Well, I did.
And I'm not apologizing. I'm tired of apologizing for shit I'm not sorry for or that I have no control over.
(*Mimicking* STEWART)
From the bottom of our hearts we apologize for our father' behavior.
(*Beat*)
Behavior that you provoked. Oh and here's five hundred dollars.
Go!

(STEWART *hurries out of the room.* JOSIE *goes to her father and holds his hand. She whispers something to him.*)

STEWART: She's down the hall in another room.

JOSIE: Then why didn't you get her?

STEWART: Because she's working. Look, she's not the person we want. We should just focus on Georgia. And leave that girl alone.

JOSIE: No. We're not leaving her alone. Especially after I got a good look at her. You notice that tattoo on her neck? I think they get those in prison.

STEWART: Neck tattoos?

JOSIE: It's a prison thing. I'm sure of it.

STEWART: It's her son's name.

JOSIE: It's still a prison tattoo. What do you wager that I'm right?

STEWART: I don't bet.

JOSIE: Good. Because you would lose. She got that tattoo in prison. I'm right. Nursing homes–

(STEWART *gives* JOSIE *a look.*)

JOSIE: Assisted living centers hire ex-cons and felons as nurses' aides all the time. Cleaning piss and shit. Nobody wants to do that. And Carly-Ann says—

STEWART: Carly-Ann?

JOSIE: Miss Olson's daughter. Carly-Ann says we have to be vigilant.
Not so trusting. And she was right.
I was too trusting.
I'm gone for one week and all hell breaks loose.
They change his caretaker.
Shit comes up stolen.
He gets taunted, then has a meltdown.
One week.
They waited until I wasn't around and they made a change without consulting me.
They could have called me, even.

No.

This is bullshit.

I'm going to find that girl. What room did you see her in?

STEWART: Across from the nurse's station. It has a rocking chair with a scarecrow sitting out front.

JOSIE: I'll see if she's still there.

(JOSIE *leaves the room.* STEWART *is alone with his dad. He doesn't know what to do. He just sits in a chair and stares at him for a long, awkward spell.*)

NURSE: *(Over the intercom)* T'Wana Jepson, please come to the nurses' station. T'Wana Jepson, please come to the nurses' station.

(JOSIE *hurries back into the room…setting* STEWART *free.*)

JOSIE: She's on her way.

And guess what? I saw her. Georgia!

STEWART: Did you say anything?

JOSIE: I wanted to so bad but I didn't want to tip her off.
(Pumps her shoulders. Ready for action)
I'm about to kill two birds with one stone. Watch me.

(JOSIE *notices* MR TURNER *is looking at her.*)

JOSIE: Daddy.
(She hurries to him.)
Are you comfortable? Everything okay?
(She tends to him, massaging his legs.)

(*After a beat,* T'WANA *comes in. She carries a stack of bath towels.*)

T'WANA: *(To* JOSIE*)* What are you doing?

JOSIE: Taking care of my father.

T'WANA: I know but you shouldn't do that. You could give him blood clots.

(JOSIE *stops.* T'WANA *goes into the bathroom to put up the towels.*)

(JOSIE *pulls out her cell phone and starts scrolling.*)

(T'WANA *comes out of the bathroom and starts out the room.*)

STEWART: T'Wana…we need your help.

(JOSIE *gives the phone to* STEWART)

STEWART: Do you know this woman?

(T'WANA *studies the image on the phone.*)

T'WANA: That's Miss Georgia.

(JOSIE *closes the door.*)

JOSIE: There's theft taking place.

T'WANA: You think it's Miss Georgia?

JOSIE: Well you can see with your own eyes.

STEWART: How well do you know Georgia?

T'WANA: She's my play mama. And I know she ain't no thief. You got the wrong person.

JOSIE: She's the only person on camera at the scene of the crime.

T'WANA: What crime?

(STEWART *looks at his sister.* JOSIE *flips through the scrapbook and finds a picture.*)

STEWART: This is our mother. This picture was taken in 1991 on my parent's twenty-fifth wedding

anniversary. She is wearing a diamond brooch that was my father's anniversary gift to her.

JOSIE: My mother's jewelry was given to charity, except for the brooch. My father kept that. When he passes it goes to me. And now it is missing.

STEWART: We put the brooch on this shelf in the white box next to my parents' picture. See on the video. She's at the shelf standing right in front of the white box. But due to the angle we can't really make out if she took it.

JOSIE: But I know she did.

T'WANA: The bottom drawers on that shelf is where we keep his underwear and stuff.
Just look like she's getting underwear out to dress your dad. Don't look like nothing bad to me.

STEWART: But she never takes out underwear. She doesn't dress him.

JOSIE: Let's watch it again.

(Quiet. They study the screen intensely.)

STEWART: See. What are her hands doing?

JOSIE: And she's standing too close to actually open the drawers.
Plus she came into my father's room without permission. She's not even assigned to this wing. I checked. And when she left the room she bumped into one of my friend's whose mother is in this wing. Miss Georgia had a weird-guilty look on her face.

T'WANA: That still don't mean she stole anything.

STEWART: When you go to that shelf we can see you opening the dresser drawers. Working. Helping our father. Everytime. That's not what Miss Georgia does.

(They look at the phone.)

STEWART: She right here. She's doing something with her hands.

JOSIE: She's taking the brooch. That's what she's doing.

T'WANA: … …If it was so important why didn't you keep it at home?

STEWART: It's our father's wish to have the brooch always by his side.
He made us promise…
…when he started getting ill.

JOSIE: What if we never get it back?

(A beat)

T'WANA: I'm sorry. I'm really sorry.
I hope you find it.
(Another beat. Then she gets up to leave.)

JOSIE: You won't help us?

T'WANA: I ain't got no help to give. And I don't care how it look on the video. Miss Georgia doesn't steal. And why would she steal that of all things? I know it has sentimental value. But how would she know it's/ worth stealing.

JOSIE: Well if she's noseying around and she sees a beautiful/ diamond

T'WANA: It looks plain to me.

JOSIE: AND SHE SEES A BEAUTIFUL DIAMOND BROOCH, she might be prone to think it's worth stealing. And please don't cut me off again.

T'WANA: You cut me off first.

JOSIE: Don't tell me I/ did.

STEWART: Josie, please…just be quiet for a moment and let me talk.
(Beat)
T'Wana, we do not want to fight. He just need your help.

T'WANA: Proverbs twenty verse seventeen says, bread gained by deceit is good to a man, but afterward his mouth will be full of gravel.

JOSIE: What does that mean?

T'WANA: It means I don't want no parts of this.

STEWART: Please don't mention to Georgia that we had this discussion.

JOSIE: Of course she's going to say something to her.

T'WANA: No I'm not. I don't even know what to say. "Mama, these white people think you're a thief."

JOSIE: Honey—

T'WANA: My name ain't honey. It's T'Wana.

JOSIE: T'Wana, everybody that came into my father's room last week was being recorded. You included.

T'WANA: So. I ain't got nothing to hide.

STEWART: We have very troubling footage of you.

T'WANA: Like what?

JOSIE: *(Mumbles to herself as she searches her phone)* Wednesday. September 25…three twenty three. There it is. See.

(They watch the video.)

STEWART: Can you explain what happened there?

T'WANA: I stuck my tongue out.

JOSIE: At who?

T'WANA: At your dad.

JOSIE: Twice.

STEWART: Two days before that we have you on video giving my father the finger.

*(*JOSIE *finds the video. They watch.* JOSIE *begins to tear up.)*

JOSIE: I don't wanna see no more.
(*She puts the phone away.*)

(*Beat*)

T'WANA: He treats me ugly. Sometimes he calls me a monkey. I don't like that. One time he called me a monkey coon. Then he spit at me.

STEWART: He's seventy-three years old and he has Alzheimer's. He's not in his right mind. You said it yourself.

JOSIE: There's also the incident in the dining room. We have witnesses.

T'WANA: You mean when he bit me?

JOSIE: He was acting in self-defense. You provoked him. So he bit you.

T'WANA: I never touched him.

JOSIE: But your actions were threatening.

T'WANA: He was cussing me. And I did this.
(*She gives* JOSIE *a "Talk to the Hand"*)
I was just trying to make him stop.

STEWART: And that's why he bit you. You put your hand in his face.

JOSIE: He took that as a threat. And I can file a report. I have witnesses that say your behavior was aggressive. Plus we have the video from his room.

T'WANA: That's not fair. He talks to me like shit. Calling me a coon, and monkey, and ni—

STEWART: We know what he called you. No need to repeat it.

T'WANA: Can't just take that and not feel nothing.

JOSIE: It's your job. If you don't like it, get a new one.

(*Beat*)

T'WANA: LaToya asked to be reassigned to another resident. She couldn't take your daddy no more. Nobody likes working with him.
(*She storms out of the room.*)

(*A long beat*)

STEWART: He's gonna get kicked out. I know it.
(*Beat*)
Josie. You went too far.
I was trying to keep her on our side. We need her on our side now more than ever.

JOSIE: I don't want her on our side. I just want her out of here. And I want Georgia out of here, too.
(*Beat*)
If you want to keep playing the nice guy, fine by me. I will gladly play the villain. Let me do the dirty work. I have no problems with that.

(*A beat.* JOSIE *waits on a response from* STEWART. *Nothing comes*)

JOSIE: Typical. Not surprised. It all falls on me. It all falls on me.
(*She slumps into a chair.*)

STEWART: Josie.
Josie.
Jo-Jo.
I'm sorry.
Jo-Jo…what would it take for me to convince you—

JOSIE: He cannot stay with me. I did the best I could. It was too much.

STEWART: I can hire a home health aide. Twenty four/ seven

JOSIE: We tried that already. It didn't work out. I don't like a stranger living in my home.

STEWART: Just give it one more chance.

JOSIE: And if it doesn't work out, then what? We uproot him again?

STEWART: If you have full-time help, it will work out. I promise.

JOSIE: No. Ask Alison if she wants a stranger living in your house.

STEWART: We can't keep him. We travel.

(JOSIE *gives* STEWART *a look.*)

STEWART: Business travel.

JOSIE: If you hire someone twenty-four seven what difference does it make if you travel?

(STEWART *doesn't have an answer*)

JOSIE: It all falls on me.
(Beat)
Go home, Stewart. Just let me handle this like everything else.

STEWART: Jo-Jo, we're in this together.

(JOSIE *doesn't respond. She keeps searching.*)

STEWART: You find it yet?

(No response)

STEWART: Jo-Jo.

JOSIE: I haven't found it yet. But I will. And stop calling me Jo-Jo.

STEWART: We agreed to settle this quietly.

JOSIE: I didn't agree to that.

STEWART: Yes you did.

JOSIE: Well I changed my mind.
Stewart, if we let this slide, daddy is going to be a target for all kinds of abuse.

STEWART: Alison said that if we're perceived as troublemakers that will make things more difficult for him.

JOSIE: For somebody who never lifts a finger to do a damn thing, your wife has an awful lot to say.

STEWART: Alison tried. You know that.

JOSIE: Your wife doesn't want to be bothered and I can't say that I blame her.

STEWART: Josie, daddy needs to come home. He doesn't have much time. Do you want him to die in this place?

JOSIE: That's ugly and unfair.

STEWART: Josie—

JOSIE: Try to guilt me into doing something you're not/ willing

STEWART: It's not about guilt.

JOSIE: You're not going to intimidate me into doing something I don't want to do. You want to intimidate somebody, do it to the folks who deserve it. Make these people do the right thing.
Stewart…
This is the best place we could find. We read all the reviews. We toured the place three times. Even had a meal with the residents. I met Carly-Ann and Simone and some of the others….
If we can't trust that, then….
Our duty is to make sure our father is treated with respect and professionalism, regardless of his State of mind. Or his actions. He could be the most racist, K K K, backwoods redneck, Neo Nazi loon in the building. None of that should have any bearing on how he is treated.

Period. We must address these issues with management. The theft, that girls' nasty behavior. These things need to be brought to their attention.

STEWART: Jo-Jo, I hear what you're saying. But I just want to keep this private.

JOSIE: Why?

STEWART: I'm worried.

JOSIE: There's nothing to be worried about.

STEWART: They'll file a report and there will be all sorts of documentation/ and

JOSIE: So!

STEWART: And there will be some sort of investigation.

JOSIE: What's wrong with that?

STEWART: She's going to defend herself. She's going to bring up all sorts of horrible things daddy has said and/ done

JOSIE: That doesn't matter.

STEWART: It matters to me.

JOSIE: He's sick.

STEWART: But that doesn't/ change

JOSIE: It changes everything.

STEWART: I don't want that being documented. I don't want him to be remembered that way.
I don't want stuff like that put on paper. We have to protect his name. What he stood for.
(Beat)
Josie, these are good people. At their core, I sincerely believe this. And I don't think anyone here would purposefully do anything to harm him. And have you seen any physical signs of abuse on daddy's body?

JOSIE: No. Not yet. But if we let them get away with this, then the word will be out. You can do anything to that man in E204 and his family won't do a thing. His family doesn't care. And as soon—

STEWART: We do/ care

JOSIE: And as soon as that gets out, just watch, that's when the real abuse starts. We have to make this visible. We have to set an example. If something happens to daddy because we did nothing, I will never forgive you—
Are you willing to take that chance? I'd rather his name be dragged through the mud than he be abused and mistreated—

STEWART: If I thought he was truly in dan/ger

JOSIE: You saw what she did.

STEWART: I don't think she is a violent/person

JOSIE: How can you know that?

(MISS GEORGIA *comes to the door and knocks.*)

MISS GEORGIA: Hi. Is it okay if I come in?

STEWART: Sure.

(MISS GEORGIA *comes in. She heads over to the bed to check on* MR TURNER.)

JOSIE: Have you been assigned to this room? Usually it's the Mexican lady or the young girl.

MISS GEORGIA: No. I work on the other side. But when things get slow on my end, I like to come over here and check on my friend.
(*To* MR TURNER)
Hey partner, how you doing? Are these your kids?
(*She goes to wash her hands and put on gloves*)
I recognize y'all from them pictures over there on that dresser.

STEWART: I'm Stewart. This is my sister Josie.

MISS GEORGIA: Nice to meet you. I'm Georgia.
Oh-Oh.
I think he just did something.
(She sniffs the air)
Your daddy needs changing.
The nose knows.
Is it okay if I take care of him now?

STEWART: Of course. You need help?

MISS GEORGIA: Naw, I'm good.
I think he waits for me before he does his business. He
likes me.
*(She reaches her hands under the blanket, slides a towel
underneath MR TURNER and begins to undo his adult
diaper. She uses a modesty cloth as she changes him)*
Wooooooooooo. You cutting up tonight, my friend.
What they feeding you?

*(MR TURNER opens his eyes. He looks at MISS GEORGIA but
he doesn't say anything)*

MISS GEORGIA: Awwwwww hell. I done woke you up.
And you ain't ever gonna let me hear the end of it. Or
you?

(T'WANA comes in)

MISS GEORGIA: But you feel better now. Don't you?
Hey, T'Wana girl. Come over here. I got a present for
you.

T'WANA: I don't want that.

MISS GEORGIA: I'm just messing with you. Come over
here, help me finish changing.

*(T'WANA washes her hands and puts on gloves. She gets a
diaper and goes to MR TURNER.)*

NURSE: *(Over the intercom)* East Wing. Code Blue. East Wing Code Blue.

MISS GEORGIA: Oh shoot. I gotta go.
Nice meeting you folks.

(MISS GEORGIA rushes out. T'WANA finishes changing MR TURNER. JOSIE goes to her father. She strokes his hair and kisses his forehead. MR TURNER gives his daughter a blank stare. T'WANA notices this. She finishes up and takes the diaper outside the room to dump it. She comes back in and washes her hands.)

T'WANA: I want to apologize for my actions. I was wrong to make faces at your father and give him the finger. I teach my boys to respect their elders. I would be embarrassed for them to know I did something like that.

STEWART: We accept your apology.

JOSIE: So does that mean you will help us find out what happened?

T'WANA: I don't really know how I'm supposed to help you.

JOSIE: Get her to admit to you that she took it. Get details. Details to prove it's true.

T'WANA: Miss Georgia is like a mama to me. She's always been there for me. I can't spy on her.

STEWART: I understand. I do and we don't want to get Georgia in trouble. My intention is to keep this very private. Just between the four of us. I promise.
(Beat)
Miss Georgia, from what I just saw is an awfully sweet and kind woman. She doesn't come off as the kind of person who would steal.

T'WANA: I been saying that.

STEWART: But sometimes things happen in our lives that cause us to do desperate things. Like steal.

T'WANA: I don't care what you say. That ain't her.

STEWART: It's not her. I believe you. But it could be her circumstances causing her to do things she might not ordinarily do. Maybe there is some burden she's carrying, and hiding. Something she needs help with and my mother's brooch looked like easy money.

T'WANA: Her son always helps her when she got money problems.

STEWART: Maybe it's more than he can help with. Whatever it is needs to be uncovered. It might be something we can help with. It might be something you can help with. You said she's always been there for you. Here's your chance to be there for her.

JOSIE: My brother is being very generous and kind in offering to deal with this in a Christian manner. I think it is in your best interest to give him the help he needs. Otherwise, my way of dealing with the situation is to pull the video images of you and file abuse charges and get to the bottom of things through an investigation. You need to ask yourself if protecting a friend is worth losing your job.

STEWART: T'Wana, you have a very important decision to make.
Would you like to have a word of prayer?

(T'WANA *accepts his hand.* JOSIE *is hesitant at first. He gives her a look, and then she gives her hand in prayer. During the prayer,* JOSIE *is quiet, but* T'WANA *nods in agreement and occasionally says "yes Father God." Her eyes tear up during the prayer.*)

STEWART: Heavenly Father, we come to you in prayer on behalf of our sisters in Christ, T'Wana and Georgia.

Lord, we don't know what they're going through, but we know that you do. And we ask that you step in and guide us to be the act of change that brings new life, hope, and prosperity to their lives.

Lord, we pray that you use Josie and me. We pray that you work through us to be the blessing T'Wana and Georgia need to move forward in life. And Lord, we ask that what is done in the dark is brought to the light. And that once it is out in the open, we will attack that demon with your Holy power, and return your children to you. We ask all these things in the matchless name of Jesus Christ. This we pray in your son's name. Thy will be done. Amen.

T'WANA: Amen.

(End of scene)

Scene Two

(Three days later. MISS GEORGIA sits in a storage room, alone. She has about thirty dollars' worth of ones and fives stapled to her scrub above her left breast. It is her birthday.)

(A bag from the Olive Garden sits on the floor beside her and a can of Big Red soda sits next to that. She reads the Dallas Morning News. After a moment, T'WANA comes in the room.)

T'WANA: Hey mama. What you doing in here? They got cake in the break room.

MISS GEORGIA: I had some already. You get some?

T'WANA: Not yet. But I was gonna get some of the girls together so we can sing Happy Birthday to you.

MISS GEORGIA: First shift already sung to me. I got here early.

T'WANA: Oh. But I want to sing to you.

MISS GEORGIA: Ain't nothing stopping you.

T'WANA: I don't want to sing by myself. Mama, why you sitting here all alone?

MISS GEORGIA: I ask Maggie if I can have some quiet time for my birthday. Get away from the other girls. But you know I don't mind you. Sit with me. Keep mama company on my birthday.

T'WANA: Yes ma'am.

(MISS GEORGIA *has the only folding chair.* T'WANA *starts to sit on the floor.*)

MISS GEORGIA: Don't sit on that dirty-ass floor. Get some of them boxes or something.

(T'WANA *finds a small box and sits on it*)

MISS GEORGIA: That's better.
(*She continues to read the paper.*)

T'WANA: Mama, whatchu reading?

MISS GEORGIA: What I always read.

T'WANA: Awwwwww hell, mama.

MISS GEORGIA: I read the obituaries every day.

T'WANA: But not on your birthday. Mama, that ain't right.

MISS GEORGIA: It is kinda messed up, ain't it?

(MISS GEORGIA *and* T'WANA *laugh.*)

MISS GEORGIA: You want some of my lunch?

T'WANA: No, I'm fine. I had some left-over Subway.

MISS GEORGIA: You sure? I only ate this little bit. You can take the rest home to your boys.

T'WANA: You don't want no more?

MISS GEORGIA: No. My son loves Italian. But somehow
he forgets I'm not big on Italian. So guess where he
takes me for my birthday? Olive Garden.
(She notices a long red welt above T'WANA's *left wrist.)*
That's not where you got bit, is it?

T'WANA: No. I got this today. I was helping to take
Miss Cohen back to her room. She got real far this time.
That old lady can run. But we stopped her 'fore she got
to the door, praise God. That alarm gets on my nerve.

MISS GEORGIA: I done told you this once already. This
is the last time I'm gonna tell you. Next time she get
to running, don't you go after her. Let somebody else
chase her down. Because that's how you get written up
for sure. 'Cause it's hard to restrain them when they
get like that. Nurses' station say you were too rough.
But they skin like tissue paper. Just slide off in your
hand. I'm telling you some good shit.

T'WANA: Yes m'am.

MISS GEORGIA: Look out for T'Wana. 'Cause this job
don't care. Don't be stupid. You better hear me.

T'WANA: I hear you—
But sometimes these folks get rough, no matter what
you do.

MISS GEORGIA: Not with me.

T'WANA: Mama, these old folks ain't never tried to
fight you?

MISS GEORGIA: Oh noooooooooooooooo. When I get
my people, first time they try and buck at me. Uh-
uh. I look them right in the eye and I tell them all the
same thing. I don't care if you got the alls-timers. The
dementia. The bipolar. Whatever. I hate that for you. I
really do. But I'm a grown-ass woman.

And if you haul off and bite, scratch, kick, or hit
me, then I'm gonna slap the piss out of you. They
understand that real good. I don't have no problems.

T'WANA: I just try and not let it get to me. I pray the
Blood of Jesus and turn away.

MISS GEORGIA: I'd be praying the Blood of Jesus
too while I'm sitting up in the jailhouse after I done
slapped the piss outta somebody.

(MISS GEORGIA *and* T'WANA *laugh.*)

T'WANA: Mama, don't go to jail behind these white
folks.
(Chuckles)
Praying the Blood of Jesus in jail.

MISS GEORGIA: I'm something. Ain't I?

T'WANA: Yes you are.

(MISS GEORGIA *and* T'WANA *just laugh. And laugh)*

T'WANA: Ooooooooh mama you crazy. Mama, did you
steal a brooch out of Mr Turner's room?

MISS GEORGIA: Did I what?

T'WANA: I'm sorry. I feel stupid asking. But it's been
killing me. I couldn't hold it in no more.

MISS GEORGIA: You think I stole something?

T'WANA: I don't think you stole anything. I know you
don't steal.

MISS GEORGIA: Then what you ask me for?

T'WANA: Mr Turner's kids think you stole from his
room.

MISS GEORGIA: Me? Why me?

T'WANA: They hid a camera in the room, and it looks
like you stole it from the dresser.

MISS GEORGIA: Shit. I knew something was up. The way his daughter talked to me. I just knew. Goddamn!
(Beat)
When you find this out?

T'WANA: Friday.

MISS GEORGIA: That's why she was giving me them nasty looks.
(Beat)
Wait a minute! You just walking around here knowing these people think I stole something, and not tell me.

T'WANA: You were off this weekend.

MISS GEORGIA: You could have called me.
Why the hell didn't you call and tell me these goddamn white people on my ass?

T'WANA: I didn't know what to say. I was caught off-guard.

MISS GEORGIA: Who all know?

T'WANA: They wanna keep it quiet. I'm the only person who knows. They don't want a big mess. They just want the brooch back and an apology.

MISS GEORGIA: You believe that?

T'WANA: That's what they said. They seem like honest people. The son prayed with me.

MISS GEORGIA: Say what?

T'WANA: Oooooooooh mama! That white man can pray. He pray like black people pray. I felt the spirit. He made me cry.

MISS GEORGIA: Made you cry?

T'WANA: He got to talking about what's done in the dark and casting out demons and the tears just started

pouring down my face. Pray like my mama used to
pray. Pray like you pray.

MISS GEORGIA: Well good for him. I hope he save some
of them prayers for his own soul. Dumping his poor
daddy off in a place like this. Mr Turner deserves
better than this. Shit! You know I look out for that man.
He my favorite one. I would never do anything against
him. Ever. Now his children on the other hand. That's
a different story. They can all go to hell.

T'WANA: Mama!

MISS GEORGIA: And that son. He the one that hurts
the most. Used to be all up under his daddy. You see
Mr Turner, you see that boy. They was each other's
shadow. I never would have thought. And how come
he all up in here now because a damn brooch done
turned up missing? Where was his ass for the last six
months? Huh? He should be ashamed of himself.

T'WANA: It's not your place to punish him.

MISS GEORGIA: It's my place to do whatever I goddamn
choose. And if you knew Mr Turner like I do, you'd
be angry, too. He gave my boy his first job. I told
you that. Changed Donald Ray's life. That's a Godly
man. First time I laid eyes on him in this place, I just
about broke down crying. All he's done and this is
how he gets treated. He was written up in the paper
on many occasions. Iola Johnson and Clarice Tinsley
interviewed him. Shit, he made Clarice Tinsley cry.
On the six o'clock news. Had that woman crying like
a baby. That's how Godly he was. And this is how he
gets to spend his final days. I'mma make sure I treat
him right.

T'WANA: Mama, all you need to do is stay the hell
outta his room. Leave him alone. He not assigned to
you. Why you look after Mr Turner like you do?

MISS GEORGIA: Looks like I got my *good white man* and you got yours.

T'WANA: What's that supposed to mean?

MISS GEORGIA: Everybody needs a good white man in their corner to get by in this world. I thought you knew that.

T'WANA: Yeah? What can he do for you laid up in that bed?

MISS GEORGIA: It ain't about what he *can* do. It's about what he did. And what that means to me. He looked out for me and my boy. And now I gotta look out for him. Do right by him. Somebody gotta do right by him.

T'WANA: So you're telling me that you didn't take the brooch?
They have you on camera.

MISS GEORGIA: You really think I did it?

T'WANA: No…but…I just wanted you to know they/
have you

MISS GEORGIA: Does it show me taking the brooch?

T'WANA: No.
(Beat)
Well you can't really tell.

MISS GEORGIA: This is some kinda birthday.
(Beat)
You think I took that shit, don't you?

(T'WANA doesn't answer.)

MISS GEORGIA: Awwwwwwww hell. Little girl, I gotta go. I can't believe this.
(She stands.)
I'm a child of the king. I don't have to steal. So you just go on believing whatever the white folks tell you.

T'WANA: Mama no…. Mama… I was just telling you what they said. That's all. But they have video and mama, one way or the other, you're gonna have to deal with them. They mean business.
Especially his daughter.

(MISS GEORGIA *considers, then reaches into her bosom and pulls out the brooch. She places it on the table. Quiet.* T'WANA *stares at the brooch in disbelief.*)

T'WANA: I thought you said you didn't steal it? Mama you lied to me.

MISS GEORGIA: I didn't steal the brooch. Mr Turner gave it to me. He said I could have it.

T'WANA: I'm sorry but that don't sound right to me.

MISS GEORGIA: That's what happened.

T'WANA: They not gonna believe that.

MISS GEORGIA: I'm not a thief. I don't steal. That was a gift from Mr Turner.

T'WANA: A gift for what?

MISS GEORGIA: I think he likes me. He thinks I'm cute. He wants to court me. He wants to be my boyfriend.

(MISS GEORGIA *chuckles.* T'WANA *ain't laughing*)

MISS GEORGIA: Hell I don't know. That's as good a guess as any.
One day when he was in his right mind and was talking normal.

T'WANA: He never talks normal.

MISS GEORGIA: When he first got here, he was talking normal…sometimes. Before the allstimers took that from him, too.
(Beat)
And one day, when he was talking normal I got real curious and asked him what was in that pretty white

box I always see. He told me to open it and find
out. And I did and saw it and I told him that it was
the most beautiful thing I'd ever laid eyes on in my
entire life. That if I lived fifty more years I'd never see
anything more beautiful. That's when he told me I can
have it. Just like that.

T'WANA: He has Allstimers.

MISS GEORGIA: I know that.
I didn't want to take it. I said I couldn't. It was too
beautiful for me to take from him. And when I said
that tears started welling up in his eyes. He started
crying. He begged me to take the brooch. He said that
I deserve to have nice things. That it would break his
heart if I didn't take the brooch. If I didn't take it then
we couldn't be friends anymore. So I pretended to take
it. I put it in my pocket and when he closed his eyes I
put it back.
(Beat)
But last week, after he bit you... I just realized how
bad he's slipping.
How fast.
How far away he is from who I remember...
And I thought back to him begging me. And I didn't
want to let him down.
So I came back and took it.
He said he wanted me to have it!
It's the last thing I remember of when he was who he
was.

T'WANA: Mama, you know I love you...but... just turn
it back in and apologize. They won't be mad.

MISS GEORGIA: That's a lie. They just said that to trick
folks. And you fell for it.

T'WANA: Why do you carry it on you?

MISS GEORGIA: I been planning to put it back, and then I have a change of heart. It's a gift. I have to keep it. This brooch could be a financial blessing that I'm giving away—

T'WANA: Or it could be the cause of you to lose your job. And go to jail... mama just give it back. If something happened to you, I don't know what I would do.

MISS GEORGIA: If something happened to me because of this brooch, because you turned me in, you wouldn't be able to make it here no how. 'Cause nobody would trust a snitch ever again. Remember that.

T'WANA: Mama, I'm not gonna turn you in.

MISS GEORGIA: Shhhhhhhhhhhhhhhhhhhhhhhhhhh. You getting too loud.

T'WANA: Maybe you can just go and slip it back where you got it from.

MISS GEORGIA: I told you. He gave it to me. And I'm keeping it!

T'WANA: They have you on video.

MISS GEORGIA: If they got me on video then they ass is in the wrong. 'Cause Texas law states you have to have a sign up in the room warning folks that you recording them. There ain't nary a sign in that whole damn room saying no such thing.
(Beat)
I checked.
So whatever they got on that video it ain't worth shit. They can't do nothing with it. And if they try some shit I can sue them for invasion of privacy. Sho can! Hell, they don't know me. I ain't the one. Shit, I been here twelve years. I know all the goddamn laws.
(Beat)

And I know how to break 'em, too.
(Beat)
Shit. Stop letting these white folks spook you. You hear me?

(T'WANA *doesn't answer*)

MISS GEORGIA: I say you hear me?

T'WANA: Yes ma'am.

MISS GEORGIA: Good.
(She considers for a moment, then prepares to leave.)
You don't know anything about this. You never saw this brooch.

T'WANA: I never saw it.

MISS GEORGIA: Promise.

T'WANA: I promise.

(MISS GEORGIA opens the door and leaves out. T'WANA paces the room for a minute to gather herself. Then MISS GEORGIA darts back in and closes the door.

MISS GEORGIA: Oh my God. Oh my God. She got security.
His daughter!

T'WANA: They said they wanted to keep it quiet.

MISS GEORGIA: White folks lie.

NURSE: *(Over the intercom)* Georgia Coleman please come to the nurses' station. Georgia Coleman please come to the nurses' station.

(MISS GEORGIA *takes the brooch out of her bosom and holds it out for* T'WANA *to take.)*

T'WANA: I don't want that.

MISS GEORGIA: Just hide it somewhere.

T'WANA: I thought you said not to let the white folks spook you.

MISS GEORGIA: What if they search me? Take it.

(T'WANA *takes the brooch*)

MISS GEORGIA: Hide it before I open the door.

(T'WANA *hides the brooch in one of the boxes.* MISS GEORGIA *leaves the room. Her phone chimes. She reads a text, then dials.*)

T'WANA: Damn.
Tramaine…is anything working…check the T V…
okay baby…baby don't start crying…mommy has everything taken care of…it's going to be okay this time…mommy has money…stop crying…Tramaine… Tramaine…listen to me…DO WHAT I SAY AND STOP TRYING TO CRY. I know it's getting dark. Take Terrell and go over to Keisha's house. What I say about the crying? Keisha won't mind. Go now before it gets **too** dark…Mama loves you, too.

(T'WANA *reaches into her pocket and pulls out her coin purse. She unzips and pulls out the holder for the debit card Stewart gave her…but no debit card. She frantically searches the purse. But no luck. Then* MISS GEORGIA *comes back into the room.*)

T'WANA: What happened?

MISS GEORGIA: I never talked to the security. Shawna said they couldn't question me without Mr Waters present.
But that woman. Josie. Oh she got hot when Shawna said that.
(*Beat*)
Where is it?

(T'WANA *drops the brooch in the Olive Garden bag.* MISS GEORGIA *quickly ties the bag up.*)

T'WANA: I have to go.
(*She starts to leave.*)

MISS GEORGIA: Where are you going?

T'WANA: Uh. I have to run home.

MISS GEORGIA: Why?

T'WANA: I misplaced something. I just remembered where I left it at the house.

MISS GEORGIA: Riiiiiiiiiiight. You hear security and you run.

T'WANA: I'm not running. I gotta pay a bill.

MISS GEORGIA: You said you misplaced something.

T'WANA: I did. My debit card…they cut my lights off and I'm trying to get them back on…. This is too much. This is too much happening right now.

MISS GEORGIA: How much do you need?

T'WANA: I **got** money.

MISS GEORGIA: Well good for you.

T'WANA: I didn't mean it like that.

MISS GEORGIA: Where you get the money from? We between paychecks.

(*A good beat*)

T'WANA: Mr Turner's kids.
It's not what you think.

MISS GEORGIA: They gave you money to snitch on me?

T'WANA: No mama. They gave me the money as an apology for what Mr Turner did to me.

MISS GEORGIA: That might be what they said. But we both know the real reason. How much they give you?

(*Quiet for a second.* T'WANA *considers a response.*)

MISS GEORGIA: How much?

T'WANA: Mama listen, give it back. Here's what you do. Tell Shawna that you want to clear your good name because you're innocent. That's what you say. Just like that.

MISS GEORGIA: I am innocent. You don't believe me. And you never answered my question—

T'WANA: JUST LISTEN TO ME. Okay. Just for a minute...you want to clear your good name. But you only want to talk to the son in private. Only the son. Stewart. And when you talk to him, beg his forgiveness and give him the brooch back. He'll let it slide. That's what you need to do.

MISS GEORGIA: How much money?

T'WANA: Five hundred dollars.

MISS GEORGIA: Well I be damn.

T'WANA: MAMA!

MISS GEORGIA: Save that mama shit for somebody else.

T'WANA: Listen to me.

MISS GEORGIA: I ain't got to listen to you.

T'WANA: Please.

MISS GEORGIA: Get away from me.

T'WANA: Listen!

MISS GEORGIA: Enjoy your thirty pieces of silver. I can't believe this shit.

T'WANA: LISTEN TO ME!
(Beat)
I'm not the one in trouble this time. You are. I'm not the one that took something that doesn't belong to me. You did. I'm not the one the police are after. And I hate that for you mama.
'Cause you won't be able to handle that kind of shit. Trust me I know. And I never thought you'd do something like this. You supposed to be setting an example for me.

MISS GEORGIA: I don't care how it looks. Lean not to your own understanding—

T'WANA: Proverbs chapter three. Verses five and six. Trust in the LORD with all your heart and lean not on your own understanding; in all your ways submit to him, and he will make your paths straight. I know my Bible. That scripture ain't got nothing to do with stealing no brooch.

MISS GEORGIA: Even if I did steal it. How can you judge me?

T'WANA: I'm not judging you—

MISS GEORGIA: You forged checks.

T'WANA: And I got caught. I paid the price. And it's over.

MISS GEORGIA: You got the nerve to judge me? You the goddamn thief. A jailbird. Not me.

T'WANA: Forget this. I'm trying to warn you and help you. And you turn on me…

(T'WANA *goes to the door to leave.* MISS GEORGIA *intercepts her.*)

MISS GEORGIA: No baby…I'm just…I'm just scared 'cause I know this looks bad. And it just hurt that you don't believe me. The point mama was trying to make is that I've always believed in /you and

T'WANA: I know/ that

MISS GEORGIA: And I've always been there for you when you been in your tight spots. And mama was just expecting that in return. Have I ever judged you—

T'WANA: You just did.

MISS GEORGIA: I didn't mean it.

T'WANA: You called me a thief.
A goddamn thief.

MISS GEORGIA: I'm sorry, baby. Can you forgive me? Pray for mama. Can you do that? Pray for mama. Like that white man prayed for you. The police were just here. Wouldn't you be scared? Maybe I took it out on you. I didn't mean to. I've prayed for you so many times…

(T'WANA *cuffs one hand behind* MISS GEORGIA*'s neck and the other hand she places on* MISS GEORGIA*'s forehead.*)

(MISS GEORGIA *raises her hands in the air.*)

T'WANA: Father God. Your child needs you right now.

(*As* T'WANA *prays,* MISS GEORGIA *says "Yes Jesus"*)

T'WANA: And Father God, we ask that you remove the spirit of mistrust, confusion and divided-ness from our hearts. We ask that you step in Lord and mend us. Mend us, Father God. Give us that perfect peace that only you provide. And we ask that you open up the hearts and minds of the Turner's so that they will see the truth that mama ain't no thief. Cause you provide over and beyond what the world can give. Cause this joy that we have, the world didn't give it and the world can't take it away. And for anyone who don't believe the words that come out of mama's mouth, Father God I ask that you provide a sign that no man can deny. A sign from Heaven above.

(T'WANA*'s phone rings. It's a Beyoncé* Halo *ringtone.*)

MISS GEORGIA: Hallelujah! Hallelujah! It is DONE! You said in your Word, Jesus.

T'WANA: Amen.

MISS GEORGIA: You promise you won't say nothing?

T'WANA: I promise.

MISS GEORGIA: Tell your babies Miss Georgia says hi. And take the rest of that Italian home. I don't want no more.

(MISS GEORGIA *leaves.* T'WANA *answers the phone.*)

T'WANA: Baby…

(*She pokes around in the Olive Garden bag and finds the brooch*)

Fuck.

(*End of scene*)

Scene Three

(MR TURNER's *room. A few hours later that same evening.*)

(*He is sleep in a big recliner—the kind they can wheel around the nursing home.*)

(MISS GEORGIA *is busy making his bed.*)

STEWART: Please.

MISS GEORGIA: I don't know what else to tell you. I am so sorry the brooch is missing. But I don't know what happened to it.

STEWART: I promise you won't—

(MISS GEORGIA *stops making the bed.*)

MISS GEORGIA: I'm tired. And I'm pulling a double tomorrow. I can't be having all this worry. The police and all.

STEWART: I did not know my sister was coming here tonight. That was not planned. My sister calls me on the phone in hysterics about you and the police. She's been calling me all night, crying and upset, and I'm just trying to get to the bottom of this so I can have some peace.

MISS GEORGIA: I need some peace too. But right now I can't seem to get it.

STEWART: If you give me the brooch, I won't make any trouble for you. I promise. I just want the – you know it's not even about the brooch anymore. I just want to get this behind us. I just want a resolution.

(MISS GEORGIA *does not respond. She goes back to making the bed.*)

STEWART: Please. Stop. Let's just talk for now. Have a seat. Right there. Just rest your feet

(MISS GEORGIA *sits on the bed.* STEWART *pulls his chair up and sits)*

STEWART: Georgia, there is no reason for you to be afraid. I'm not here to judge you or anything like that. Okay?

(MISS GEORGIA *looks at* STEWART *like he's crazy. That look that only black women can give you. He takes a breath. It's gonna be a long night.)*

MISS GEORGIA: Today is my birthday. I had to work on my birthday which is bad enough, but then I come here and get accused of things. And have the police in my face.

STEWART: I'm sorry this has to happen on your birthday.
(Beat)
Miss Georgia, may I ask, how old are you?
(Oh no he didn't)
Maybe that's not—
I am forty-seven. Are you older or younger/ than

MISS GEORGIA: I'm sixty-seven years old. I ain't shame. Young folks not making it to be half my age these days. I'm blessed and highly favored. 'Cause I serve a Living God.

STEWART: Amen. Amen.

MISS GEORGIA: Amen. Amen....? Sound like you in church.

(STEWART *smiles. Then he reaches into his wallet and starts pulling out dollars. He hands* MISS GEORGIA *a few bills.*)

STEWART: Happy birthday.

MISS GEORGIA: *(She counts the money.)* Sixty-eight dollars?

STEWART: One to grow on. That's yours to keep.

MISS GEORGIA: Why you giving me money and you think I stole?

STEWART: Because I'm a Christian.

MISS GEORGIA: Well I'm a Christian too—but damn.... You go to church?

STEWART: Yes ma'am.

MISS GEORGIA: What church you go to?

STEWART: I go to a non-denominational church. Fellowship Dallas. We have people from all different races at my church.

MISS GEORGIA: I attend Lord's Missionary Baptist Church in South Dallas. Down in BonTon we call it. Reverend Carlton Garrett was our pastor for thirty-seven years 'til God called him home. Now his grandson the pastor.

STEWART: You like the grandson?

MISS GEORGIA: He alright.
(Beat)
Your sister go to church?

STEWART: Not as much as she should.

MISS GEORGIA: Maybe that's why she so hate-filled.

STEWART: You don't know her well enough to make that statement.

MISS GEORGIA: I know enough.

STEWART: Listen. I'm giving you that money on good faith to show you that I mean you no harm. I want to help you. If you give me the brooch I won't even tell my sister you had it. I'll say it was misplaced or something. I sincerely believe you are a good woman.
(No luck)
Georgia, I prayed. Last night I prayed to God to give me guidance. And God sent me a dream. And in that dream, you took the brooch. And my grandmother was in that dream. She was in the room when you took it. And whenever my grandmother is in a dream, the dream is either true or it comes true. Now I'm not here to judge you, or punish you. I'm just here for the truth.

MISS GEORGIA: You really don't remember me, do you?

STEWART: I'm sorry, but…
Should I?

MISS GEORGIA: Well I remember you. And your father, too.

STEWART: How do you know my family?

MISS GEORGIA: My son worked for your father's moving company. My boy used to take me to the company picnics at Six Flags.

STEWART: And?

MISS GEORGIA: And.
That's it.
You and your daddy used to serve all the employees food at the picnic. You served the hot links. He served the brisket. Your mother served her famous sweet tea. But I never got in her line. It was always too long. But they say that was some real good tea. I never saw your sister. I went every year for five years. But I don't remember seeing her.

STEWART: That's how I'm supposed to remember you? I served you hot links at our company picnic?

MISS GEORGIA: I was just another face in the crowd, I suppose. I don't guess you would remember me. But I'll never forget your family and I will never forget what your daddy did for my son. Turned his life around.

My boy Donald Ray had some run-ins with the law and nobody would hire him. A sister at my church said to take Donald Ray down to Turner's on Lamar and he'll take care of him. We went down to see your daddy, explained the situation and your daddy hired him on the spot.

STEWART: No questions asked. Right?

MISS GEORGIA: Right. How you know?

STEWART: He did that for a lot of people.

MISS GEORGIA: That's the kind of man your daddy was. Ha! They don't make 'em like that anymore.
(Beat)
Oh well, look like it's almost time for me to go home. Gotta finish this shift.
Wanna help get your daddy in the bed?

(STEWART helps MISS GEORGIA lift MR TURNER into bed)

MISS GEORGIA: Your father. He was so proud of you. Still is.
I'm so happy you're here. He's missed you so much. He'd call out your name. Wishing for you. But he never blamed you. He blamed himself.

STEWART: What are you talking about?

MISS GEORGIA: You were in college and one day you brought a beautiful black girl home. You wanted her to meet him your father because you were proud of him and everything he stood for. And you wanted him to be proud of you, too. But your daddy had been catching hell because of his policies, losing business, losing friends, and when he saw you with that black girl something snapped. He asked you to follow him to the kitchen, and he called her a Nigger Bitch so loud, that when you went back into the other room, she was gone. He couldn't live with that for a long time. If he had just called her one word or the other word, it wouldn't have been as bad. But he called her a Nigger—Bitch. Both words. And it kills him...because he doesn't remember her name. And he'll never remember her name. But he remembers those words he called her. Tell him her name. He wants to know her name before he dies.

STEWART: Paulette.

MISS GEORGIA: Such a pretty name. Paulette.

(MISS GEORGIA *starts to leave when* JOSIE *charges into the room. She looks wrecked.*)

JOSIE: You get the brooch? She confess yet?

(STEWART's *mind is somewhere else.*)

JOSIE: Stewart?

STEWART: Jo-Jo. I think we need to leave.

JOSIE: Leave? I'm not going anywhere/ until

STEWART: We need to talk through this further.

JOSIE: I'm done talking.

STEWART: Josie.

JOSIE: Everybody in this nursing home is conspiring against us. They don't want us to know the truth. (*Gets in* MISS GEORGIA's *face*) Just admit you stole my daddy's shit.

STEWART: JOSIE!

MISS GEORGIA: I'm going back out on the floor. Shawna said if you keep harassing me, then she's calling security.

You causing a disturbance.

(MISS GEORGIA *goes to the door.* JOSIE *blocks it*)

MISS GEORGIA: Tell her to move.

STEWART: Josie. Please move.

JOSIE: No. I'm protecting daddy. If we let this/ slide

(There is a knock at the door.)

T'WANA: Is everything okay? Mama? It's me.
(She comes inside.)
Mama, Mr Hinton smells real bad. I need help
changing him.

JOSIE: We're having a discussion with Georgia. It's not
over.

MISS GEORGIA: Yes, it is.

T'WANA: We need to change him before shift ends. Or
we'll get wrote up.

JOSIE: Why can't you do it by yourself?

T'WANA: He's too heavy.

MISS GEORGIA: She ain't got to explain nothing to you.
Let's go. I'm reporting you to the nurses' station.

(MISS GEORGIA *and* T'WANA *start to leave. But* JOSIE
blocks the door.)

JOSIE: *(To* T'WANA*)* Why did you run off today?

T'WANA: What?

JOSIE: I saw you in the parking lot. You ran to your car
and drove off. After the police came. Why did you run?

T'WANA: It was an emergency. I had to go home.

MISS GEORGIA: I said, you don't owe her no
explanations.

JOSIE: She can't talk for herself?

What made you run so fast? Getting rid of the evidence?

STEWART: Huh?

JOSIE: You stole from our father. But you were going to let Georgia take the blame. Weren't you?

T'WANA: No. I did not steal—

STEWART: Okay. Now I'm really confused.

JOSIE: She's a thief. An ex-con. I ran a background check. She stole people's identity. She forged checks. She did time in the pen. I told you she did time.

MISS GEORGIA: T'Wana they're running a game on us. Probably trying to collect some insurance or something. We not stupid. Don't let them scare you.

JOSIE: Shame on you, letting this poor innocent woman take the fall.
(*To* MISS GEORGIA)
We owe you an apology.

MISS GEORGIA: You don't owe me a damn thing. Cause I know this ain't nothing but a trick.
T'Wana!
Come 'on!

JOSIE: You walk out that door and I'll press every charge in the book.

MISS GEORGIA: T'WANA!

(T'WANA *stays puts.* MISS GEORGIA *storms out.*)

STEWART: T'Wana, why didn't you tell us about your background?

(*Long beat.* T'WANA *doesn't answer*)

STEWART: T'Wana.

T'WANA: What difference does it make?

STEWART: I mean if you have a history of theft….

That changes… it makes me…

…T'Wana, I don't want to believe that you stole from
my father. But some things my sister has said make
sense. And that troubles my soul. See, I prayed last
night to God to give me guidance. And God sent me
a dream. And in that dream, you took the brooch.
And my grandmother was in that dream. She was
in the room when you took it. And whenever my
grandmother is in a dream, that dream is either true
or it comes true. T'Wana, God is moving through this
room right now,

(JOSIE *rolls her eyes.*)

STEWART: and he is unleashing a spirit of forgiveness,
Renewal. Wholeness. But T'Wana, these things have a
price. They don't come free and the price is the truth.

JOSIE: The truth is you're about to lose everything. Your
job. Your freedom. Your boys.

STEWART: Josie, you're not helping.

JOSIE: Let me finish.

T'Wana, I know you care about Georgia. I know you
want to look out for her. But you have to look out for
your boys, first, above all else. Look out for yourself
and your own best interest because your babies
depend on it.

T'Wana…

What happened to your boys when you were in jail?

T'WANA: They were put in foster care.

JOSIE: How old were they?

T'WANA: Six and four.

JOSIE: I'm sure you worried about your sons every
single day you were in jail, but especially with them
being in foster care. Yes? Being away from your sons
and not knowing how they're being cared for, if they're

being abused. If they're scared. And you can't help them. And when you remember the way you felt then, that's the way we feel about our father. The same fear. And can you remember how much you would have given every second of the day just to know your boys were safe. If you remember those things then you have to help us. Tell us the truth. Tell us what you know, an we'll know that our father is safe. Because good people look after him.

T'WANA: I wish I could help you. But I don't know anything.

STEWART: T'Wana, God delivered you and he delivered your boys too. Do you believe that?

T'WANA: Yes.

STEWART: Deep down in your heart. Do you really believe?

T'WANA: Yes! I do.

STEWART: God brought you back to your boys. God did that. Georgia didn't do that. She's been there for you, I'm sure. But that one thing that you wanted most. She couldn't give that to you. God did. And who is going to help you turn your life around? Georgia can do a lot. But she can't do what God can do.
And just think, anything could have happened to your boys in foster care. But God kept them.
T'Wana this is your chance to show God your faithfulness and gratitude for your family's deliverance. This is your chance.

(Beat. No response from T'WANA.)

JOSIE: How long were you in prison?

T'WANA: Sixteen months.

JOSIE: Your babies were in foster care for sixteen months?

T'WANA: No. Eight months.

JOSIE: I thought you/said

T'WANA: Miss Georgia got the courts to let her take custody.

I'm sorry…I can't…

(*She rushes out of the room.*)

JOSIE: That's it Stewart. We lost. It's over.

STEWART: Jo-Jo, don't say that.

JOSIE: It's gone Stewart. We just have to accept it.

(*Outside, Miss Cohen runs past the door. Someone hustles ass to get her. She screams. More commotion outside*)

JOSIE: I hope she gets away. I hope she leaves this horrible place.

I don't blame her. I'd run, too.

Run Miss Cohen. Ruuuuunnnnnnnn!

Stewart…

I want us to move daddy. I don't want him here anymore.

He's not safe here.

This is a horrible place.

STEWART: Well where do we move him to?

(*Beat. No answers from either*)

STEWART: Jo-Jo, we're out of options.

(*A long beat passes as the truth settles in.*)

(*The door opens. It's* T'WANA. *She quickly closes the door.*)

T'WANA: You promise I won't get in trouble, right? YES?

STEWART: Yes. I promise.

(T'WANA *reaches into her pocket and pulls out the brooch.*)

(*She gives it to* STEWART.)

T'Wana: And I can explain.

Stewart: No. No explanations. It's…
Okay.

T'Wana: I just want you to know…I didn't steal that. I found it last week when I was going through a basket of dirty towels in the laundry room. I didn't know who it belonged/ to

Josie: Why didn't you just turn it in?

T'Wana: You're right. I should have just done that.

Josie: Then why didn't you?

(T'Wana *doesn't answer*)

Josie: Why didn't you say something when we came to you?

(*A beat*)

T'Wana: I was afraid you'd think I stole it.

Stewart: But we know that you didn't. And we thank you for doing the right thing.
(*He looks at his sister.*)

Josie: Thank you.

T'Wana: I appreciate you understanding.
(*She leaves.*)

Stewart: Thank you, Jesus.

Josie: You know she was lying.

Stewart: It doesn't matter.
(*He heads for the dresser drawer*)

Josie: What are you doing?

Stewart: I'm putting this back where it belongs.

Josie: Have you lost your damn mind? After all we've been through.

(MISS GEORGIA *rushes in. She stands at the doorway and watches.*)

STEWART: It's not going to turn up missing twice.

JOSIE: Oh you're right about that. Because it's coming home with me.
(*Sees* MISS GEORGIA)
Can we help you?

(MISS GEORGIA *doesn't answer.* T'WANA *comes into the room.*)

JOSIE: Can we help you?
Is there a problem?

MISS GEORGIA: That brooch belongs to me.
Your father wants me to have it.

T'WANA: Awwwww hell. Mama.

MISS GEORGIA: It's true. They ain't got no rights to it. And he don't want it no more.

JOSIE: I want you to leave our room.

MISS GEORGIA: It's not your room. It's your daddy's room. And he's fine with me here. We friends, like I said.

JOSIE: I'm going to ask you one more time. Please leave us alone.

MISS GEORGIA: I'm not leaving 'til I get what's mine.

JOSIE: I'm calling the police.

T'WANA: Whoa. Whoa. Whatchu calling the police for?

JOSIE: Criminal trespassing.

T'WANA: I gave you what you wanted. Please don't call the police.

JOSIE: She won't leave our room.

T'WANA: Mama! Let's just go!

MISS GEORGIA: They not walking out of here with what belongs to me.

JOSIE: Now she's physically threatening us.

MISS GEORGIA: I ain't got to lay a hand on your ass. 'Cause I got truth on my side.

(STEWART *puts the brooch in his pocket.*)

STEWART: Josie, we're going home. We have the brooch. That's what we wanted. We're going home.

JOSIE: I'm not leaving them alone with daddy.

STEWART: It's over. We can go now.

(STEWART *starts to move but* JOSIE *stays put.*)

STEWART: You want to stay. Stay. But we got what we came for and I'm done.

(STEWART *starts out.* MISS GEORGIA *rushes to him.*)

MISS GEORGIA: Listen. Listen. Listen.
Come on, let's talk for a minute please. We can work something out.

STEWART: Something like what?

MISS GEORGIA: I don't have a lot of money to buy it. I'm sure it cost a fortune—

T'WANA: Mama. Don't you dare.

MISS GEORGIA: You keep out of this.

STEWART:	MISS GEORGIA:
It's not /for sale	Just hear me out.

JOSIE: You couldn't afford it anyway.

MISS GEORGIA: I KNOW THAT! But listen. Listen. I can work it off.

T'WANA: Mama, you're embarrassing yourself.

MISS GEORGIA: Say one more goddamn word to me.

STEWART: What exactly do you have in mind?

JOSIE: Are you fucking kidding me?

STEWART:	JOSIE:
How much do/you make here?	No.No.No.No.No.No.

MISS GEORGIA: Twelve twenty-five an hour.

STEWART: Benefits?

JOSIE: I don't want her in my home.

STEWART: She's really good with daddy.

JOSIE: She's a thief. A thief, Stewart. T'wana told a lie to protect her.

STEWART: What makes you think it was a lie?

JOSIE: I'm not stupid. And neither are you.
I don't want a thief in my home.

MISS GEORGIA: He's safer with me than he is with you.

JOSIE: What the hell is that supposed to mean?

MISS GEORGIA: What do you think it means?
Does your brother know?
About the burn?

(A beat. JOSIE isn't quick with a comeback.)

(Another beat passes.)

STEWART: What burn?
T'Wana, you can go now. This no longer involves you.

MISS GEORGIA: They don't need you anymore is what he's saying. They used you. And you let them. Just plain stupid.

(T'WANA leaves the room.)

STEWART: Josie. What is she talking about?

(STEWART waits for an answer. Nothing comes.)

MISS GEORGIA: Your daddy got a real bad burn on his bottom. First time I saw it. I went straight ahead and reported it to the nurses' station. 'Cause I didn't want nobody to get wrote up behind that shit. Lose they job. Because I could tell it wasn't fresh. It had been there for a while. And when I reported, the charge nurse told me it was already in your daddy's files. They did documentation on day one when you brought him here.

Don't believe me, I can go get the files right now and show you. They took pictures and everything.

STEWART: Josie?

(JOSIE's face is tear stained. She goes to the bathroom and closes the door. STEWART goes to his father. He caresses his forehead. MR TURNER's eyes open)

STEWART: Hey daddy, how ya doing? Didn't mean to wake you. Is it okay if I check on something?

(A long awkward silence as father and son look at each other)

STEWART: How do I turn him? What's the best way?

(MISS GEORGIA comes over to help. STEWART pulls the covers down. Then he pulls his father's pajamas down, revealing a deep red burn covering most of his buttock. He goes to the bathroom door.)

STEWART: Josie. Josie. I want to talk to you.
(To MISS GEORGIA)
Can you give us privacy?

(MISS GEORGIA doesn't leave.)

STEWART: Josie…Josie… Please, Georgia. I asked you to leave.

(The bathroom door opens.)

JOSIE: Why is she still here?

MISS GEORGIA: Your daddy holding my hand tight. See. I let go what that say to him?

STEWART: *(To* JOSIE*)* You wanna step outside so we can talk.

JOSIE: No.

STEWART: I saw the burn.

JOSIE: And…
(Beat)
It was an accident. I stepped away for fifteen seconds. Just to get my head clear. He was cursing me and I needed to get those words outta my head. Fifteen seconds. It…
It— It was an accident.

STEWART: Why didn't you tell me about it?

JOSIE: Seriously?

STEWART: It looks really bad.

JOSIE: Make her leave.

*(*STEWART *gives* MISS GEORGIA *a look.)*

MISS GEORGIA: Hey friend. I have to go now. Gotta get on my rounds.

*(*MR TURNER *squeezes* MISS GEORGIA*'s hand.)*

MISS GEORGIA: I'll be back some other time.
You squeezing real tight. Hate to see me go. I know.

JOSIE: It's just some sort of reflex.
Stop pretending it means more than it does.

MISS GEORGIA: Wanna know how it happened? The burn?

STEWART: No.

MISS GEORGIA: You sure. I know because your daddy told me.

STEWART: I said I don't want to know.

*(*MR TURNER *squeezes tighter and begins to make some sort of sound. He won't let go of* MISS GEORGIA*'s hand.)*

MISS GEORGIA: One night, she was trying to give him a bath. Trying to help him get into the tub. And he cursed her.

STEWART: Please stop. NOW.

MISS GEORGIA: He called her a stupid bitch. She just shoved him in the tub and walked away. Ain't check shit!
She left him there in that hot water all by himself. And he didn't know how to get out the tub.

(*Tears run down* JOSIE's *face, again.*)

STEWART: That's enough.

MISS GEORGIA: And the water started burning him bad. And he started/ screaming

STEWART: I said stop.

MISS GEORGIA: I'm not finished.

STEWART: Stop Goddammit!

(STEWART *goes to comfort* JOSIE.)

MISS GEORGIA: He could have drowned.

JOSIE: He—
(*She can't get the words out.*)

STEWART: Josie. It's okay. It's okay.

MISS GEORGIA: Is that what you wanted? For him to drown!

STEWART: Leave my sister alone.

MISS GEORGIA: Let him drown. So you won't have to be bothered with him anymore. Ungrateful children just cast their parents aside. You'd be happy if/ he was—

JOSIE: I wouldn't let my father drown. I love…
(*More tears*)

MISS GEORGIA: That's why he gave the brooch to me. He said you don't deserve anything belonging to your mother.

(JOSIE *charges toward* MISS GEORGIA. *But* STEWART *intercepts his sister.*)

STEWART: Josie, its okay. I know you love daddy. You love him so much and you would never do anything to hurt him.

(JOSIE *sits in a chair. She tries to gather herself.*)

STEWART: Get out of our room.

(MR TURNER *is still gripping* MISS GEORGIA's *hand.*)

STEWART: I've tried to be fair. But you're taking advantage of us.

MISS GEORGIA: How am I taking advantage of you?

(JOSIE *rushes over to* MISS GEORGIA.)

JOSIE: Let him go!

(MISS GEORGIA *gently pulls herself from* MR TURNER's *grip.* JOSIE *takes her place, holding her father's hand. He continues to make sounds.*)

JOSIE: Daddy? Daddy? What's wrong?

(MR TURNER *lets out a series of anguished cries.*)

(T'WANA *rushes in.*)

MISS GEORGIA: Don't hold his hand that way.

JOSIE: Why?

MISS GEORGIA: Because I said so.

T'WANA: You're hurting him.

STEWART: Josie, just let them handle it.

JOSIE: You get away from my father. Don't touch him.

MISS GEORGIA: You're making it worse.

STEWART: Josie!

T'WANA: Shit. He's bleeding.

MISS GEORGIA: You tore his skin.

JOSIE: I didn't do anything.

MISS GEORGIA: His skin like tissue paper. I said you was holding him wrong.

(T'WANA *gets the first aid kit and starts to nurse on* MR TURNER *who moans and wails.*)

MISS GEORGIA: Everything gonna be alright, partner. We got you.

(JOSIE *tries to help.* MISS GEORGIA *elbows her away.*)

MISS GEORGIA: Please come get your sister.

JOSIE: I wanna help.

MISS GEORGIA: NO.

STEWART: Josie, just get back.

JOSIE: Don't tell me what to do.

(JOSIE *forces her way back in.* MR TURNER *sees her and cries out more.*)

JOSIE:	MISS GEORGIA:
Daddy!	Get away!

STEWART: Jo-Jo!

MISS GEORGIA: Leave him/ alone

JOSIE: NO!

(MISS GEORGIA *gets in* JOSIE's *face.*)

MISS GEORGIA: LEAVE HIM ALONE!
HE'S AFRAID OF YOU!
HE HATES YOU!

(JOSIE *slaps the piss out of* MISS GEORGIA. MISS GEORGIA *takes a second to recover from the surprise and shock. Then she gets a look in her eyes. But before she can charge* JOSIE,

T'WANA *pulls* MISS GEORGIA *back into the opposite corner of the room.)*

(MISS GEORGIA *finally feels the sting of the slap. She slumps into a chair. Her nose is bleeding.)*

T'WANA: Mama. It's cool. It's cool. She ain't worth it.

STEWART: Josie. Go out and wait for me in the parking lot.

(JOSIE *sees all the blood and hurries out of the room.* STEWART *closes the door behind her.)*

STEWART: My sister got carried away. But that wasn't her fault. You provoked her—

MISS GEORGIA: Yea? But I'm the one bleeding.

STEWART: *(To* T'WANA*)* You saw her provoke my sister.

(T'WANA *doesn't respond. He reaches into his wallet)*

STEWART: We can make this right. Okay. Would two hundred dollars—

T'WANA: You gave me five hundred.

MISS GEORGIA: I don't want your goddamn money. I want the brooch.

STEWART: I'm sorry but I can't do that. Just take the money.

MISS GEORGIA: No.

STEWART: Then you need to go now.
There's nothing else I can do.
I've gone above and beyond.

MISS GEORGIA: Really?

STEWART: Yes. I have.

(STEWART *goes to* MR TURNER. T'WANA *nudges* MISS GEORGIA *to leave. But she doesn't.)*

STEWART: Why are you staring at me like that?

(MISS GEORGIA *stares* STEWART *down for a long beat.*)

STEWART: If you don't leave I'm reporting you to management.

MISS GEORGIA: I ain't 'fraid of management.

STEWART: Then I'll call security.

MISS GEORGIA: Call security.

STEWART: How 'bout I call the police?

T'WANA: Shit!

STEWART: I don't want to call the authorities but I will if I have to.

(*A long stand-off*)

(*If looks could kill* STEWART *would be dead.*)

T'WANA: Please. Mama.

(STEWART *pulls out his phone.*)

MISS GEORGIA: You calling the police on me and I'm the one that was attacked?

STEWART: I've given you fair warning.

MISS GEORGIA: White folks call the police for the stupidest shit.

(MR TURNER *begins to makes noise, again.* T'WANA *tries to calm him with no success.*)

STEWART: You're upsetting my father.

MISS GEORGIA: No. You're upsetting him.

(MR TURNER *grows louder.*)

T'WANA: Mama!

(STEWART *starts dialing.*)

STEWART: I'm dialing.

T'WANA: Mama! Let's go!

(T'WANA *is about to bail but* MR TURNER *grabs* T'WANA's *arm and pulls her close.*)

MR TURNER: (*Sweetly*) Paulette.
Paulette.
Paulette.

(MR TURNER's *grip on* T'WANA *intensifies. She winces. She tries to pull away. This upsets him.*)

(*His tone changes.*)

MR TURNER: Paulette
Paulette

(T'WANA *tries to pull away again.* MR TURNER *grits his teeth.*)

MR TURNER: Nigger Bitch!
Nigger Bitch!

(T'WANA *finally pulls away.* MR TURNER *begins to cry like a baby.*)

(STEWART *is frozen. Watching his father sob. Then he hurries out of the room.*)

(MR TURNER *is wailing like a baby.* MISS GEORGIA *doesn't move to quiet him but his crying becomes so bothersome that she has no choice. She goes over to calm* MR TURNER.)

(*She succeeds.*)

(*An uncomfortable stretch of quiet.* T'WANA *examines her arm.*)

(MR TURNER *scratched* T'WANA. *But didn't draw blood.*)

(MR TURNER *has shit himself again.* MISS GEORGIA *starts to tend to him.*)

T'WANA: You need help?

(MISS GEORGIA *doesn't answer. She just proceeds with the process for cleaning and changing his diaper, using the modesty cloth. A moment passes.*)

T'WANA: Mama?

MISS GEORGIA: Don't talk to me. Don't say a goddamn word to me. I'm done with you.

(MISS GEORGIA *continues her task.* T'WANA *sits. Quiet*)

T'WANA: I was trying to stop them from calling the police.

MISS GEORGIA: I said I'm done with you.

T'WANA: You started all of this.
As soon as they said the police, that should have been the end of it.

(MISS GEORGIA *finishes up the diaper change. She dumps the diaper.*)

MISS GEORGIA: Like this piss and shit I'm dumping in the trash, that's our relationship.

T'WANA: I don't deserve that.

MISS GEORGIA: You don't deserve.
You fix your mouth to tell me what you don't deserve.
I went through all kinds of shit for you and your boys.
I got talked to all kinds of crazy. Got treated like I was the criminal.
I put up with all of it.
And it wasn't fun. And it wasn't pretty. And it wasn't easy. And it sho as hell wasn't cheap.
Two extra mouths to feed, that I couldn't even afford.
And I didn't even think twice about it.
But all you had to do was keep your goddamn mouth shut.
And you couldn't even do that.
You couldn't do that for me.

T'WANA: I didn't even say your name. I took the blame.

MISS GEORGIA: I don't care.

T'WANA: I took the blame for something you did. It
could've gotten me in a world of fucking trouble. And
you don't care?

MISS GEORGIA: That one perfect, beautiful thing
And it was mine.
Don't I deserve that much?
I ain't worth that?

T'WANA: I'm talking 'bout my sons having a mama
who can tuck them into bed at night, and all you care
about is a piece of jewelry?

MISS GEORGIA: You the one let it get all carried out of
proportion. I asked you to do one thing.

T'WANA: I did what I had to do. T'Wana gotta look out
for T'Wana. Ain't that what you said?

MISS GEORGIA: After everything I've done for you. You
just threw away the only thing you and your boys had.

T'WANA: Me and Tramaine and Terrell—
We all you got too.
(Beat)
Your son got that nice house out in the country. In Red
Oak. Good job. His wife got a good job.
Why you don't live with them?

MISS GEORGIA: I choose to live by myself. I like my
independence.

T'WANA: In the projects.

MISS GEORGIA: I don't live in the projects.

T'WANA: Next door to the projects. Close enough. Why
he let you live in a bad neighborhood?

MISS GEORGIA: It's not a bad neighborhood.

T'WANA: Police sirens every night. Burglar bars on
every window. Every door. When I was ready to move
you begged me to stay.

MISS GEORGIA: I didn't beg /you

T'WANA: You did too beg me because you were afraid to live alone. You cried when they put you on this shift because you were afraid to go home alone after dark. And Donald Ray knows how bad that neighborhood is. But he just left you there anyway. You needed me just as much as I ever needed you.

MISS GEORGIA: My son loves me. He takes care of me. Give me anything I need.

T'WANA: A couple of dollars here and there. Lunch on your birthday to a place you don't even like. You're sixty-seven years old. If he loves you so much how come he lets you work your fingers to the bone cleaning shit for a living?
(Beat)
I used to feel sorry for these people living here. But now I don't know which is worse. Making your mother live in a nursing home, or letting your mother work in one.

MISS GEORGIA: I still got some of your clothes at my house. Some pots and pans too. And some bullshit odds and ends you gave me for Mother's Day. Tonight when I get home, I'm gonna take your clothes, put everything in a box and set it outside my front door. And anybody who wants to pick through it is free to it. And you left your boys' birth certificates in a zip-lock bag and that's going out on the street with the rest of your shit too. So I suggest you come get it if it means anything to you. Because it don't mean a damn thing to me anymore.

T'WANA: I'll be there first thing in the morning.

MISS GEORGIA: Shit might be gone by then.

T'WANA: I'll take my chances.

(T'WANA *starts to leave, when all of a sudden—an alarm goes off. There is a commotion outside in the parking lot.*)

(*Outside,* Miss Cohen *shouts.*)

(T'WANA *looks out of the window. A slight smile stretches across her face.*)

(T'WANA *turns to see* MISS GEORGIA, *slumped in a chair. Tired*)

(*Resting*)

(T'WANA *sits.*)

(*Her shoulders relax.*)

(*She takes a breath.*)

(*Now a car alarm goes off.*)

(*More commotion*)

(*But the ladies sit motionless.*)

(*Outside in the parking lot,* Miss Cohen *laughs triumphantly.*)

(MISS GEORGIA *and* T'WANA *lift their heads.*)

(*They let out a breath.*)

(*Their eyes meet.*)

(MISS GEORGIA's *nose is bleeding again.*)

(T'WANA *offers her some tissue.*)

(MISS GEORGIA *hesitates, then accepts.*)

T'WANA: Look up.

(MISS GEORGIA *tilts her head up.*)

(T'WANA *is gentle as she wipes* MISS GEORGIA's *bloody nose.*)

(*Lights fade to black.*)

END OF PLAY

www.ingramcontent.com/pod-product-compliance
Lightning Source LLC
Chambersburg PA
CBHW052213090426
42741CB00010B/2518